UNSOLVED QUESTIONS ABOUT LIVING THINGS

BY CAROL KIM

CAPSTONE PRESS
a capstone imprint

Published by Capstone Press, an imprint of Capstone
1710 Roe Crest Drive
North Mankato, Minnesota 56003
capstonepub.com

Library of Congress Cataloging-in-Publication Data
Names: Kim, Carol, author.
Title: Unsolved questions about living things / by Carol Kim.
Description: North Mankato, Minnesota : Capstone Press, an imprint of Capstone, [2023] | Series: Unsolved science | Includes bibliographical references and index. | Audience: Ages 8–11 | Audience: Grades 4–6 | Summary: "How did life begin? How many species are on our planet? Can we bring extinct species back to life? When it comes to life on our planet, there are a whole lot of questions we're still trying to answer. Get ready to explore the unknown and discover how scientists are working to solve the mysteries of living things."—Provided by publisher.
Identifiers: LCCN 2022025116 (print) | LCCN 2022025117 (ebook) | ISBN 9781669002444 (hardcover) | ISBN 9781669002390 (paperback) | ISBN 9781669002406 (eBook PDF) | ISBN 9781669002420 (kindle edition)
Subjects: LCSH: Life (Biology)—Juvenile literature.
Classification: LCC QH501.K55 2023 (print) | LCC QH501 (ebook) | DDC 570—dc23/eng/20220611
LC record available at https://lccn.loc.gov/2022025116
LC ebook record available at https://lccn.loc.gov/2022025117

Editorial Credits
Editor: Christopher Harbo; Designer: Sarah Bennett; Media Researcher: Svetlana Zhurkin; Production Specialist: Katy LaVigne

Image Credits
Alamy: AGAMI Photo Agency, 14, Moviestore Collection Ltd, 16; Associated Press: San Francisco Chronicle/Jerry Telfer, 26; Capstone: Jon Hughes, cover (bottom left), 18; Getty Images: Jose Luis Pelaez Inc, 20, Mark Garlick, 8–9, Ralph White, 10, 11; Shutterstock: Achiichiii, 23 (top), aslysun, 4, atanasis (background), cover and throughout, BlueRingMedia, 25, Christoph Burgstedt, 7, Corona Borealis Studio, cover (bottom right), Dennis van de Water, 19, Dr Morley Read, 12, Dr Project (background), cover and throughout, fluidmediafactory, 27, Gorodenkoff, 17, joshimerbin, 21, K.K.T Madhusanka, 23 (bottom), Natalia Kuzmina, cover (top), nobeastsofierce, 24, O.Pash, 29, Panagiotis Komninelis, 28, View Apart, 15, vitstudio, cover (bottom middle), Westlight, 6; Smithsonian Institution: National Museum of Natural History, 9 (inset); Superstock: Minden Pictures, 13

Printed and bound in China 5132

TABLE OF CONTENTS

INTRODUCTION
The Mysteries of Life 4

CHAPTER 1
How Did Life Begin?. 6

CHAPTER 2
How Many Species Are There on Earth? 12

CHAPTER 3
Can We Bring Extinct Species
Back into Existence?. 16

CHAPTER 4
Where Did Viruses Come From? 20

CHAPTER 5
Can We Learn to Communicate with Animals? 26

Glossary. 30
Read More 31
Internet Sites 31
Index 32
About the Author 32

Words in **bold** are in the glossary.

THE MYSTERIES OF LIFE

The work of scientists will never be done. Every day is spent asking and answering new questions. Our curiosity helps us learn more about the world around us.

Some questions can seem silly, such as, "Which came first, the chicken or the egg?" But even silly questions are worth pondering. In fact, the chicken or egg question has been tossed about for centuries. Even the famous Greek **philosopher** Aristotle spent time thinking about it.

| Whether in labs or out in the field, scientists continue to look for answers to life's many unsolved questions.

So, what's the answer? An egg probably came first, because the chicken had to come from somewhere. What many scientists believe is that an almost-chicken-type bird laid an egg. Inside that egg was a bird with a **genetic** change that made it into a full chicken.

Science has solved many mysteries. But there are still questions that remain unanswered. Here we explore some questions about the world of living things that continue to stump scientists.

THE SCIENTIFIC METHOD

Scientists use a process called the scientific method to answer unsolved questions about living things. They follow these steps:

- Ask a question
- Gather information
- Make a prediction
- Design an experiment to test the question
- Collect data
- Analyze data
- Draw conclusions
- Communicate results

CHAPTER 1

HOW DID LIFE BEGIN?

At some point, more than 4 billion years ago, Earth formed. To begin with, it was a huge mass of dust and gas. No living **organisms** existed at that time. But very, very slowly, conditions on the planet changed. Somehow, from nonliving matter, the first living organisms formed. How did this change come about?

| In its earliest form, planet Earth was a super-hot ball of molten rock lifelessly floating in space.

Scientists can only make educated guesses about how life first began. Most scientists believe life couldn't have begun until some key building blocks were in place first. These include **amino acids** and **RNA**. Amino acids help build the **proteins** living cells use to perform functions. RNA transfers genetic information into proteins.

| As shown in this illustration, amino acids link together in chains to build proteins.

FACT Proteins are found in every cell in your body. They are needed to build and repair your muscles and tissues and keep them all working correctly.

| The building blocks of life may have come from volcanic gases or from meteorites during Earth's early formation.

One theory is that life began on Earth in areas near volcanoes. The mixture of gases and heat may have helped create the earliest life-forms. Volcanoes spewed high amounts of sulfur dioxide into the air. Chemicals called sulfites probably began gradually forming. When mixed with water, these sulfites could have created the building blocks needed to form RNA.

| The Murchison meteorite, which fell in Australia in 1969, is famous for the amino acids found inside it.

Another theory suggests life may not have begun on Earth at all, but out in space. Life-forms from another planet could have been brought to Earth on board a comet or meteorite. In 1997, some evidence of this theory was found. Scientists discovered amino acids deep inside one meteorite that landed in Australia in 1969.

A third theory is that life began on the ocean floor near hydrothermal vents. These vents release a rich mix of heated chemicals and **minerals**. Some scientists believe chemical reactions between these elements created cells. These cells would have been the earliest forms of life.

| Black smokers release dark, mineral-rich plumes of material from chimney-like vents on the ocean floor.

However life began, many scientists agree on one thing. The first forms of life would have been simple, single-cell organisms, much like **bacteria**.

LIFE AROUND HYDROTHERMAL VENTS

Hydrothermal vents are like hot springs produced by underwater volcanoes. They are located deep on the ocean floor. Temperatures in the vents reach up to 750°F (400 °C). The pressure at this depth is also intense. Yet the areas around the vents are rich with life. Fish, clams, shrimp, and strange tube worms make their home around the vents.

| Colonies of snakelike tube worms sway in the super-heated water near a hydrothermal vent.

CHAPTER 2

HOW MANY SPECIES ARE THERE ON EARTH?

You might think counting, or even estimating, the number of different **species** on Earth would be easy. But even today, the answer is simply unknown. Different estimates have ranged from 5.3 million to 1 trillion species. That's quite a large spread!

| Counting the number of plant and animal species living in just one section of a rain forest would be difficult. Just imagine trying to count them across the entire planet!

Many species are hard to discover because they are so difficult to reach. It is hard to explore places like the ocean's depths, remote areas, and high up in the tallest trees. And some categories of living things, such as insects, also contain huge numbers of species.

FACT In 1979, beetle expert Terry Erwin discovered more than 1,100 new species of beetles in Panama. They were all in the tops of just one group of trees!

| Terry Erwin uses biodegradable pesticide to collect and study insects living in the rain forest canopy.

In 2011, a group of scientists came up with a new way to calculate the number of species. They started with a system of classifying living things invented about 250 years ago. For the first time, scientists were able to agree on a number that they believed was fairly accurate.

Using this new system, they calculated the number of species on Earth at 8.7 million. Scientists also estimated that 86 percent of all land and 91 percent of all ocean species remain unknown. With so many undiscovered species, it could take more than 1,000 years to finish recording them all!

| The blue-throated hillstar is a species of hummingbird that was first discovered in Ecuador in 2017.

CLASSIFYING AND COUNTING LIVING THINGS

The system scientists use to classify living things places them into seven main groups. Starting broadly with kingdoms, the groups become increasingly narrow, with the smallest grouping being species. For humans, the first group is the kingdom Animalia and the last is the species *Homo sapiens*.

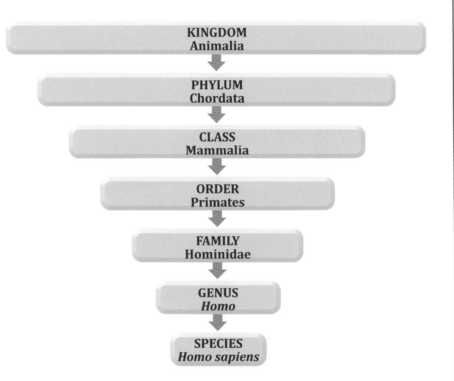

KINGDOM
Animalia

PHYLUM
Chordata

CLASS
Mammalia

ORDER
Primates

FAMILY
Hominidae

GENUS
Homo

SPECIES
Homo sapiens

Using patterns between the number of organisms in each group, scientists can now guess how many species are likely to live on our planet.

CHAPTER 3

CAN WE BRING EXTINCT SPECIES BACK INTO EXISTENCE?

In the movie *Jurassic Park*, scientists brought dinosaurs back from extinction. This idea, while exciting, seemed very far-fetched. But it's actually a lot closer than it used to be.

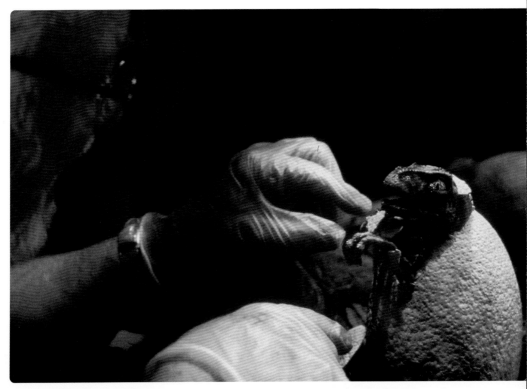

| *Jurassic Park* provided an exciting, fictional vision of what it might be like to bring dinosaurs back from extinction.

| Scientists use the latest advancements in technology to help them unlock the secrets of living things.

Because of advances in science, bringing back extinct animals has become more possible than ever before. Scientists can now take **DNA** from the preserved remains of animals that no longer exist. DNA is genetic material that has information about how a living thing will look and behave.

New experiments are already being attempted. Scientists are trying to place DNA from one extinct species into a closely related living species. The goal is to produce offspring that have the extinct species' DNA.

| Woolly mammoths were similar in size to African elephants, but they had long fur and much longer tusks. Some woolly mammoth tusks grew up to 15 feet (4.6 meters) long!

Using this method, one group of scientists is trying to bring back the woolly mammoth. This animal last roamed Earth 4,000 years ago. Woolly mammoth DNA is taken from **fossils** of their remains. The DNA will then be added to Asian elephant cells, the closest related living species.

If successful, the result would not be a true woolly mammoth. Instead, it would be something like a **hybrid** elephant. It would have some characteristics of its ancient cousin, such as long, shaggy fur. Scientists working on the project are calling the hoped-for animal a "mammophant."

CAN DINOSAURS BE BROUGHT BACK?

In *Jurassic Park*, dinosaurs were brought back to life. While DNA can be collected from fossils, it has a limited shelf life. Samples can last thousands of years. But more than a million years is pushing it. Dinosaurs have been extinct for about 65 million years. Unfortunately, the DNA of a *Tyrannosaurus rex* has long since expired.

| It's fun to imagine bringing a *T. rex* back to life, but expired DNA will likely keep this old fossil frozen in time.

CHAPTER 4

WHERE DID VIRUSES COME FROM?

You know about the common cold, the flu, and COVID-19. They are all caused by viruses. But there are many, many more viruses on our planet. In fact, there are more than a quadrillion quadrillion of them. That's at least 5 to 10 million times more viruses than stars in the universe!

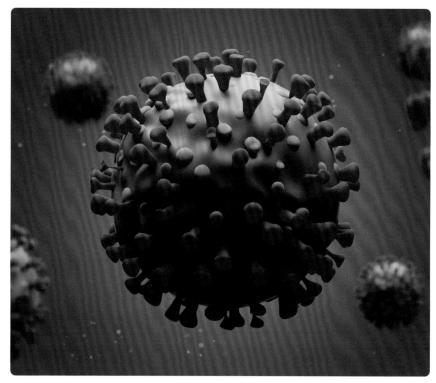

| The outside of the COVID-19 virus is covered in spike proteins that allow the virus to invade living cells and cause illness.

Viruses are a type of germ. They can only live and reproduce inside another living cell. But where did they come from? Believe it or not, the answer is still a mystery.

FACT The word *virus* comes from Latin. It means "poison" or "slimy liquid." No wonder it's the word we use for something that makes us sick!

There are three main theories about where viruses first came from. One theory is that viruses came before cell life. This is the "virus first" **hypothesis**. It suggests that viruses must have come before cells because they have a simpler structure. Viruses may have served as a base from which more complex cells later developed.

Another theory is called the "regressive" or "reduction" hypothesis. It suggests that viruses started out as regular cells. These cells began to enter larger cells—perhaps to share resources. Over time, they relied more and more on their host for survival. Eventually, they stopped being able to survive on their own.

FACT The origin of viruses is difficult to trace because there are no virus fossils. Viruses are simply too small and fragile to be preserved.

ANIMAL CELL STRUCTURE

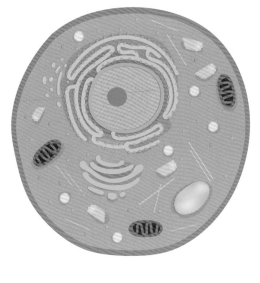

TYPICAL VIRUS STRUCTURE

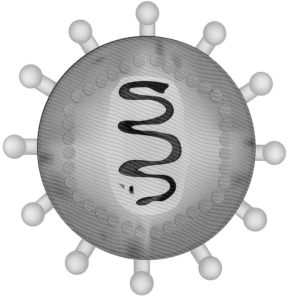

| Compared to an animal cell, the typical virus has a much simpler structure with far fewer parts.

The third model is called the "escape" hypothesis. Viruses could have started from pieces of genetic material that broke off from early cells. The pieces then entered other cells and needed those host cells to survive.

Right now, scientists remain divided over which theory is most likely correct. In fact, scientists disagree on many things when it comes to viruses. There isn't even agreement about whether viruses are living things or not.

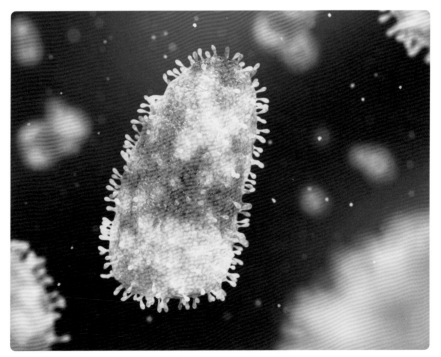

| At the microscopic level, viruses often look like creatures from other worlds.

ARE VIRUSES ALIVE?

Viruses are not alive. But they are not exactly nonliving, either. They have some characteristics of living things. This includes having genes and being able to reproduce. But they cannot produce energy, or reproduce by themselves. They must have a host cell to do those things.

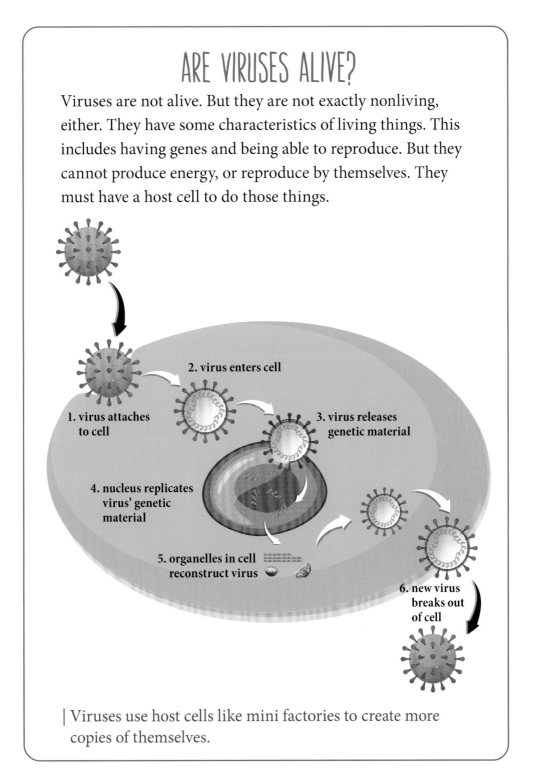

2. virus enters cell

1. virus attaches to cell

3. virus releases genetic material

4. nucleus replicates virus' genetic material

5. organelles in cell reconstruct virus

6. new virus breaks out of cell

| Viruses use host cells like mini factories to create more copies of themselves.

CHAPTER 5

CAN WE LEARN TO COMMUNICATE WITH ANIMALS?

Scientists have tried to communicate with animals for decades. During her lifetime, Koko the gorilla learned about 2,000 words of spoken English. She communicated with humans using sign language. Koko and her caretakers were able to "talk" because the gorilla could express herself using a human language.

| Koko the gorilla learned sign language from her trainer, Penny Patterson, in the 1970s.

But what about the other way around? Could people learn to speak gorilla? Could we learn dog, or dolphin, or any other form of animal communication? Some scientists believe it's possible.

Dr. Con Slobodchikoff, a professor at Northern Arizona University, has studied the language of prairie dogs for 30 years. The animals make high-pitched calls to warn others of danger. But Slobodchikoff has found that there is not just one "Danger! Danger!" call. Prairie dogs make different sounds to warn each other about different predators. They seem to be describing sizes, shapes, and even color.

Dr. Slobodchikoff is using artificial intelligence (AI) to learn the prairie dog language. AI uses computers to analyze and learn the prairie dog sounds. It can even study facial and body expressions. Dr. Slobodchikoff is studying thousands of videos of prairie dogs communicating. He hopes to translate the prairie dog language into English.

But there are limits to how well humans can bridge the communication gap with animals. It's one thing to understand danger signals. But do animals have feelings or share jokes? We may never know.

Prairie dogs may try to keep their communication secrets all to themselves, but scientists are working hard to crack their code.

Being curious helps you understand the world around you on a deeper level. When you ask questions, it leads you to explore. It often brings up more questions. Even if some questions don't have answers, there is much you can learn on your quest to find them.

FACT Studying animal languages is a growing field. Scientists are also working on projects involving sperm whales, dolphins, and even marmosets.

GLOSSARY

amino acid (uh-MEE-noh ASS-id)—a basic building block of protein that contains nitrogen

bacteria (bak-TEER-ee-uh)—very small living things that exist everywhere in nature

DNA (dee-en-AY)—material in cells that gives people their individual characteristics; DNA stands for deoxyribonucleic acid

fossil (FAH-suhl)—the remains or traces of an animal or a plant, preserved as rock

genetic (juh-NET-ik)—relating to physical traits or conditions passed down from parents to children

hybrid (HYE-brid)—a mix of two different species

hypothesis (hye-POTH-uh-siss)—an idea about how or why something happens

mineral (MIN-ur-uhl)—a material found in nature that is not an animal or a plant

organism (OR-guh-niz-uhm)—a living plant or animal

philosopher (fuh-LOSS-uh-fer)—a person who studies truth and knowledge

protein (PROH-teen)—a chemical made by animal and plant cells to carry out various functions

RNA (ar-en-AY)—a copy of DNA used to assemble proteins; RNA stands for ribonucleic acid

species (SPEE-sheez)—a group of plants or animals that share common characteristics

READ MORE

Armentrout, Patricia. *Living Things*. New York, Crabtree Publishing Company, 2022.

Marçolla, Bernardo. *Me and You and the Universe*. Minneapolis: Free Spirit Publishing, 2020.

Phillips, Howard. *Inside DNA and RNA*. New York: Rosen Publishing, 2022.

INTERNET SITES

American Museum of Natural History: Ology
www.amnh.org/explore/ology

Arizona State University: Ask a Biologist
askabiologist.asu.edu

Ducksters: Biology for Kids
www.ducksters.com/science/biology

INDEX

amino acids, 7, 9

animal communication, 26–29

bacteria, 11

cells, 7, 10, 11, 18, 21, 22, 23,
  24, 25

dinosaurs, 16, 19
DNA, 17, 18, 19

extinction, 16–17, 19

fossils, 18, 19, 22

hydrothermal vents, 10, 11

Koko the gorilla, 26

meteorites, 8, 9

origin of life, 6–11

prairie dogs, 27–28
proteins, 7, 21

RNA, 7, 8

scientific method, 5
species, 12–15, 17, 18

viruses, 20–25
volcanoes, 8, 11

woolly mammoths, 18–19

ABOUT THE AUTHOR

Carol Kim believes books and words have a magical ability to change the world, and she writes for children with the hope of spreading some of that magic. She is the author of the picture book biography, *King Sejong Invents an Alphabet* as well as more than a dozen fiction and nonfiction books for the educational market. Carol loves unearthing real-life stories and little-known facts to share with young readers. She lives in Austin, Texas, with her family. Learn more at her website: CarolKimBooks.com.